Berkshire County Library

LOCAL HISTORY COLLECTION

Library LOCAL STUDIES COLLECTION
CENTRAL LIBRARY
ABBEY SQUARE
READING
BERKS. RG1 3BQ. Tel. 509243

Class No: .H.BAS./.D.........................
942.271

FOR REFERENCE ONLY

38067005916411

D1497020

THE STORY OF BASINGSTOKE

Anne Hawker

The Story of
BASINGSTOKE

BERKSHIRE COUNTY LIBRARY

LOCAL HERITAGE BOOKS
Newbury, Berkshire

Acknowledgements

I must first thank the staff of the Record Office, Winchester, who for fifteen years have patiently found documents for me. Also the staff of Basingstoke Library, for their unfailing help in my research.

I am grateful to Eric Stokes who gave me much information about public utilities.

My thanks to the Hampshire County Museum service for permission to use several photographs from their collection in this book.

Finally I would like to thank my editor, Margaret Carruthers, for her encouragement and help with ordering my researches and committing them to paper.

RPL	Local Collection
Class	H3AS/D
Acc. No.	15526
Acc. Date	5.85

FIRST PUBLISHED 1984
© Anne Hawker 1984

All rights reserved. No reproduction permitted
without the prior permission of the publishers:
LOCAL HERITAGE BOOKS
3 Catherine Road, Newbury, Berkshire
and 36 Queens Road, Newbury, Berkshire

ISBN 0 86368 011 9

Produced through MRM (Print Consultants) Ltd., Reading, Berkshire.
Printed in England by The Wembley Press, Reading, Berkshire.

Contents

The cover illustration is of Chapel Hill and the town from the Liten. The tower of the old Town Hall is in the background.

A section of The 1762 map of Basingstoke showing the old Market Place and Town Centre.

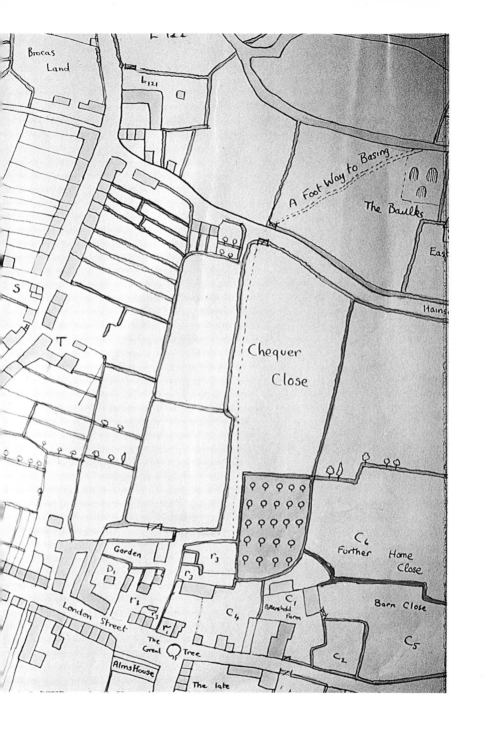

Phone Bell Carter Elliot Richards Ltd Basingstoke 57955 and we'll tell you why five world leaders spend so much time on the telephone.

Origins

About 8,000 years ago Mesolithic hunters left the first signs of life near the valley which was to become the site of the town of Basingstoke. This area of Hampshire was an area of small hills and valleys. The streams and marshes of the valleys would have provided wild birds to be trapped and fish to be speared. Deer, wild cattle and pigs lived in the forests, and there is evidence that the hunters killed these animals, for their broken flint tools have been found together with animal bones in the places where these men stopped.

One of these stopping places may have been near where now traffic lights stand where Penrith Road meets Sarum Hill. The Basingstoke historian Mr Willis discovered a large area of blackened earth and flints when he stopped to look down an excavation for a sewer there. As the ground was thoroughly burned, he thought that a hunting party had stopped here to cook their meal, using a large fire.

These hunters would have eaten, rested and travelled on, but the Neolithic men who left polished stone axes at Buckskin about 4,000 BC had begun to clear the forest. These people had become settled enough to build shelters and grow crops. They may have buried one of their tribe in the long barrow near Brackley Way. There were some more barrows, round this time, near the long barrow, but these were made some time later, after 2,300 BC.

The hill at Winklebury where a fort was built about 600 BC is about 400 feet above sea level, giving good views of the surrounding countryside. Its Iron Age inhabitants could protect themselves and their cattle against other raiding tribes behind its high earth banks which could have been topped with a palisade of sharpened stakes. There is evidence that the fort was used for about 100 years after its construction, deserted for a time and then re-occupied during the period 300 - 100 BC.

Later settlers at the time of the Roman invasion lived on other hills including Ruckstalls, Buckskin and Oakridge. These Celtic tribes were not only farmers who kept cows, sheep and pigs, but worked iron too, and wove cloth.

Two Roman oil jars were found under the remains of nine bodies in the Oakridge Well (Jefferson Road). The bodies may have been of a later period (and might possibly have suggested the name of the pub The Nine Saxons). On the north side of Oakridge Road evidence has been found of a more civilised house, in Roman style, probably built by one of the native Britons, including a bath house. When the site was excavated it was discovered to have had glass in the windows and under-floor heating. The piles of tiles that had held up the floor so that hot air could circulate were still in place and the stoke hole for the furnace was found just outside, on the west side. Other items found during the excavation were a sandal with nails in the sole and a fine grey pot. Unfortunately no coins were found to help date the site accurately.

Too far away to have been the owner, the body of a middle-aged man was found inside a stone coffin when Winklebury was excavated. Interestingly, the stone for the coffin had been quarried and transported from Bradford-on-Avon. Two coins found with the body enabled archaeologists to date the burial at between 150-170 BC.

Britain had been conquered in the Claudian invasion in 43 AD

For nearly half a century 'Lilly on the Hill' has been the Basingstoke home of Lilly Industries Limited manufacturing and marketing human and animal health care products and agrochemicals

LILLY INDUSTRIES LIMITED
Kingsclere Road, Basingstoke

under the command of Aulus Plautius,and it was to form part of the Roman Empire for the next 367 years. During this time there began to be invasions by Saxons along the south coast, especially when, in the latter years of the Roman Empire, Rome was increasingly preoccupied with its own defence against the Barbarians. After the sack of Rome in 410 AD the Saxons were able to make further incursions inland in Britain, and though local chieftains kept them back as long as they could, by 600 AD most of southern Britain was held by the Saxons.

Until recently there were very few signs of Saxon occupation in the Basingstoke area, but excavations on Cowdery Down, north of the railway line to London between Basingstoke and Basing have shown traces of hall-type dwellings. Other evidence of Saxon habitation in the area include a spearhead with a spiral decoration in yellow metal, said to have been picked up in the fields north of the first Oakridge Estate, and a beautiful bowl found when the railway was extended into Thorneycrofts.

The fine Roman towns had no place in the Saxon farming economy and were often left deserted as 'the haunt of ancient gods'. Silchester gradually decayed though Winchester continued to be occupied.

There was a complex period of transition from late Romano-British to Saxon occupation with significant numbers of the 'invaders' initially arriving as mercenaries to defend the Romano-British chieftains against attacks from Germanic tribes across the Channel. A period of invasion and settlement gradually led to a patch-

Spearhead, thought to be Saxon and said to have been found in the fields north of Oakridge Estate.

work of Anglo-Saxon kingdoms which the southern Kingdom of Wessex eventually dominated by the 9th century AD.

Saxon Wessex itself was the subject of another wave of invasions in the 9th century with the arrival of the Vikings. In 860 AD a host of Danes landed and stormed Winchester. Ten years later they took Reading and a party of them fought King Aethelred and his brother at Basing. The Danes were victorious. In 878 AD the Vikings occupied most of Wessex and only King Alfred resisted them. He finally defeated the Vikings and forced them to accept a division of England at the Treaty of Wedmore.

After a period of peace in the 10th century, the Vikings returned in 980 AD in a series of raids. Gradually larger armies were attracted by the wealth and fertility of England, and by 1017 there was a Danish king on the throne - King Canute, and England had been incorporated into the Great Scandinavian Empire. After Canute's death and burial at Winchester, disputes which arose about the Succession broke up the Empire and allowed Edward the Confessor to succeed to the throne.

In the absence of a direct heir to Edward, the Witan chose his brother in law Harold as his successor. According to Norman chroniclers, Harold had sworn on holy relics to support Duke William of Normandy's claim to the crown. It was to seize his rightful inheritance that the Duke arrived with his army in 1066. His claim was justified by force of arms at Hastings, where Harold and the cream of the Saxon ruling class were slain.

William, having taken possession of his kingdom, consolidated his victory and began to ensure its permanence by giving lands to Norman lords in exchange for military service of armed knights. A policy of rigorous suppression was accompanied by an unpre-

The Samantha Jane Collection

Lingerie & Leisure Wear Specialists
for Weddings and all
Occasions.
Stockists of
Gossard and Warners
Underwear
(A·B·C·D·DD & E Cup bras)

UNIT 3, UPPER WOTE ST. Tel: BASINGSTOKE (0256) 29624

Stone coffin and its occupant found when Winklebury was excavated.

cedented exercise in administrative efficiency.

The Domesday Book was to be a testament to the Conqueror's meticulous government. It is in this book that we first hear of Basingstoke by name.

Domesday and After

The Domesday Survey says of Basingstoke - The King holds in demesne Basingstoke. It has never paid tax nor been divided into hides. The land contains 20 ploughlands. There are 3 ploughlands in demesne and 20 villeins and 8 boors with 12 teams. There are 6 serfs and 3 mills which pay 30 shillings and 12 coliberti with 4 ploughlands. There is a market paying 30s, and 20 acres of meadow.

The first two sentences mean that the King owned the land of Basingstoke himself, and that it had not been assessed for tax, presumably because it was the property of the King. Then, the land contained 20 ploughlands. A ploughland is the amount of land that a plough team can keep in cultivation – heavy or hilly land would naturally be more difficult and take more time and effort to work – and on average the ploughland was 120 acres.

At the time of the Survey in 1086 there were perhaps 46 families in Basingstoke, most of them living in houses with closes of land around them, where they could keep hens and geese and grow vegetables and apples. They farmed the fields, but we do not know whether each man's land was scattered in the fields of the community in small strips of an acre each strip, or whether they kept their holding in one block of about 32 acres for each man. Very much later, the fields of Basingstoke *were* so divided into small strips, but there is no information about the individual possession of the men of 1086. The larger animals, the oxen and horses and cows, had to have meadow to graze, and there were 20 acres of meadow in Basingstoke. There was woodland enough to pay a tax of twenty pigs, so there were pigs and probably sheep, with their swineherds and shepherds.

There were three mills, which would have been water-mills, situated along the valley of the Loddon. One may have been in what is now Eastrop Park, for there was once a water-mill on a site where the green bank supports the footbridge over the road to Basing View. Another was at the end of Eastrop Lane, and another at the end of Essex Road, just before Victory Roundabout.

The fact that there was a market in Basingstoke at the time of the

One of the new ponds in Eastrop Park. The site of one of the Domesday water-mills is under the bridge seen across the pond beyond the large trees.

Survey indicates that Basingstoke had become the trading centre for several villages. It was in a favourable position, set on a road from London to Winchester. Basingstoke was never walled, and the nearest castle was at Basing.

There may not have been a church at Basingstoke at this time. It was not until 1155 that the Abbot and Convent of St Michael in Normandy were said to hold three churches in the bishopric of Winchester, one at Basing, one church of Basingstoke and the church of Selborne.

The King demanded from Basingstoke, Kingsclere and Hurstbourne together, one nights 'firm'. The firm was the food for one night for the whole company of the king, and would have been quantities of honey, bread, ale oxen or sheep, geese, hens, cheese, butter, salmon, fodder and eels. The King made use of these provisions as he went from place to place, these taxes in kind providing the essential supplies for the itinerant Royal court. Other landlords were often paid in kind. Some duties to the church (church-scot) were eggs at Easter and hens in the autumn. When money became of more use to the lord, money was paid instead of food or duties, and was known as 'quit-rent' i.e. they were 'quit' of the duties by money payment.

Later, instead of payment in kind, money was becoming of more use to the king, for by 1220 King Henry commanded the sheriff to deliver to Luke de Drummere the *rent* of the town of Basingstoke 'just as the men of the town have been accustomed to pay the same into our exchequer', so the 'firm' had become money. By then it was £80 for Basingstoke's share. This was apparently quite a heavy burden and the people of Basingstoke had trouble in raising it, several times being in arrears.

Many towns would rather collect their own taxes and keep the sheriff out of the town. They wanted their own court, market, fairs and tolls and were prepared to pay for these privileges. When kings needed to pay professional soldiers to fight their wars or to organise a crusade, they were open to persuasion, and took a 'gift' to grant a charter to a town. London paid a very large sum – it is said to have been £1,000 – to Richard I for a charter, but no other places were so rich.

Basingstoke continued to grow as a trading centre and market throughout the 11th and 12th centuries. Towards the end of the 12th century, Henry III needed to raise money when trying to regain lands in France. Even such a small contribution as that which Basingstoke would have been able to pay would have influenced him, for in 1256 King Henry granted a charter to the men of Basingstoke, allowing them to collect their own fines and rents, and forbidding any royal official to interfere with them. The fines and market tolls and rents made up the money to be paid to the King, and if there happened to be anything left over, presumably the men of the town could have it. Although the charter has the words 'to hold of us and our heirs to them and their heirs forever' it was prudent to get each king as he began his reign to confirm the previous charters. The charter of Henry V reviews the charters of Henry III and Edward III and confirms them. Basingstoke was to be free to keep its own customs and liberties and must pay a rent of £80 yearly to the king. The men of Basingstoke were not silent, obedient serfs any more, but business-like townsmen who wanted a voice in their own affairs.

International affairs had their repercussions in Basingstoke. As a result of King John's quarrel with Pope Innocent III, England was placed under an Interdict, which meant that all churches were closed, and no marriages or funerals could take place. Baptisms and confession of the dying were still allowed.

However, the dead must be buried, and if not in the churchyard, then another place had to be found. In Basingstoke, it was on the hill to the north of the town, now called the Liten, or corpse-ground. From 1208 to 1213 this awkward situation continued until King John needed support to regain his lands in France, and made peace with the Pope. The Interdict was lifted, the Liten was consecrated and a chapel built there.

The early chapel had thick walls of flint, probably then faced with stone, which has now gone, leaving only the flint core. The wall standing at the west end of the ruin was part of the tower of the chapel and contains a 13th century window. The door is later, 15th century. This part was used later as a school. The larger tower of creamy stone is Tudor. Near the earlier tower, within the rectangle formed by displaced tombstones is a recumbent stone figure so damaged that it is not possible to say whether it was meant to be

Hammicks in Basingstoke

CAN WE HELP YOU?

We Stock **thousands** of titles at all times including:-

☐ A huge Selection of Paperbacks
☐ Childrens Books for all ages
☐ Local Books, guides and Maps
☐ Computer Books and Software
☐ The Best of Bargain Books
☐ Leisure, business and Reference Books
☐ The Latest and Best in Hardback & Paperback Fiction
☐ Greetings cards and wrapping paper

HAMMICKS BOOKSHOPS LTD.

Personal Service and good bookselling combined at:-
WOTE ST. BASINGSTOKE. TELEPHONE: (0256) 27070

Ruins of the Holy Ghost Chapel. This early 19th century engraving shows the little footpath to the left which was to become Vyne Road.

male or female. It can only be described as an Elizabethan in a long gown. Although the face has gone, the feet are quite distinct, neatly placed together and pointing to the sky. Under the trees to the north (originally this would have been inside the chapel) is one more figure, this time definitely a knight in mail, with a long surcoat, a shield and sword. He is very much older, has lost both face and feet and has been very much knocked about. As he was discovered under the ruins of a wall in the 19th century, the falling stones probably did the damage. He is thought to be Sir William de Brayboef, Lord of the Manor of Eastrop, who died in 1284.

Associated with the earlier chapel was the Gild or Fraternity of the Holy Ghost. This was a society something like a friendly society or benefit club, the members helping each other in sickness, and as a religious society it had a chaplain, and masses were celebrated in the new chapel. There were two Wardens and an Alderman elected as well, who acted for a year at a time. The chaplain, as well as the religious service, took the duty of teaching any boys of the town Latin. The Gild possessed some property, lands and money were left them, and more money was probably raised by sales of ale at meetings, rather as we have coffee mornings today. People were still buried in the Liten as well as in or by the church in the town, but only rich men had tombstones then. The common townsman, if he had anything, would be marked with a heap of turf or maybe a wooden headboard. The road up to the chapel cut into the chalk and was sometimes known as the Whiteway. It was notorious for being so slippery in bad weather that men had to hold onto the hedges to keep upright.

Another chapel, completely vanished now, was the chapel of St John. Chapels of this sort were set up to care for the sick, and one was already established in Basingstoke when Walter de Marton enlarged and improved it about 1240. His parents lived and died in Basingstoke but he himself became a great man of the Church, Bishop of Rochester, and founded Merton College, Oxford. The site of the chapel can be seen from the shopping platform by looking over the wall of the steps opposite the Bass House. There is a municipal garden, of rocks and shrubs, and a very tall lamp standard, but no little chapel. It cannot have been very large, for two hundred years later it was said that there was an obligation for the Warden of Merton to find and maintain a chaplain, a clerk and two poor people. He had not done so, although he had received the yearly value of £5:6:8d so the king seized the revenue and only let the college have the income back when the place was properly ordered again. The chapel had the income from a house, 150 acres of land, 6 acres of meadow and 4 of pasture land in Basingstoke.

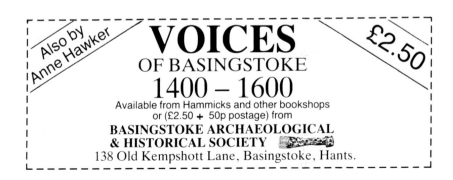

Also by Anne Hawker

VOICES

OF BASINGSTOKE

1400 – 1600

£2.50

Available from Hammicks and other bookshops
or (£2.50 + 50p postage) from
**BASINGSTOKE ARCHAEOLOGICAL
& HISTORICAL SOCIETY**
138 Old Kempshott Lane, Basingstoke, Hants.

The stone figure in the centre of the site of the schoolhouse of the Chapel School may have been of Mr Holloway who left money to help the school in 1587.

At last we hear the names of some of the inhabitants of the place; in 1207 there was 'William the Reeve', in 1275 Ralph Toke gave land at Basingstoke to Philip de Lucy, then Rector of the church of Basingstoke, in alms. Early tenants of the land later belonging to the Chapel of St John were William le Cok and Robert le Franceys.

It is also recorded that the men of the town were accustomed to meet in a meeting place called a 'clocherium' (1250) which should have meant it had a bell on it, to call them to meetings and to warn of fire or other dangers. The market day had been changed from Sunday (which was quite a usual day for a market, men should not be working in the fields and had leisure to buy and sell, but churches complained that market days became rather rowdy) to a Wednesday, every week.

During the 14th century, the Black Death took its toll of the population of England; between a third and a half of the population died. As a result of this catastrophe land was plentiful, but labour was scarce, which led to a sharp rise in wages for the labour force. The growing prosperity of the paid labourers increased the dissatisfaction of the villeins who increasingly deserted the lord's land and refused to perform their obligations to him.

This social discontent culminated in the Peasant Revolt of 1381, and peasants are said to have burned Manor Records in order to destroy the hated list of duties. Perhaps that is why there are no very early records of Basingstoke,. However, it is known that by the end of the 14th century, Basingstoke had emerged as a fully fledged market town complete with its own charter.

The Fifteenth Century

Records for the fifteenth century begin with the announcement that the King (Richard II) had granted Basingstoke a licence to become a perpetual community and to have a common seal. This was meant to be a help to them because there had been a disastrous fire in the town, so they were very poor. If they possessed a seal of their own, there would be no need to pay for the king's official seal for their legal documents.

A whole series of Court Records, known as the Rolls, begins in 1398. These Rolls were in fact rolls of parchment, and they recorded the cases brought to the town court. This court was held every three weeks, on a Saturday. Twice a year there was a special court called a Frankpledge Court. The Frankpledge was the name of the men who had sworn loyalty to the king, which they did when they were twelve years old. If boys had not come to court to swear this oath their fathers were fined 3d. Women and men in holy orders did not swear, nor did they have to be present in court unless concerned in some case before the court.

The community of men was divided into groups of ten men originally, with the headman chosen as a foreman of a jury is chosen today, to speak for the group. The whole group was responsible for the misdoings of one of them and had to pay his fine if he did not. As time went on the tithingman or head of the ten became one man from the whole village, whose job it was to answer for the village and to come to court with one or two sensible men, his associates. They reported or *presented* any misdemeanour and said who had died or come of the age of twelve or how land had changed hands. It was a current report on the state of each tithingman's own tithing.

Twice a year the tithingman had to pay a sum of money for his tithing called cert money, which was probably the same thing as the 'headpenny'. Cert money came from Chineham, Eastrop, Cliddesden, Hatch, Kempshott, Nately, Somershill, Steventon, Tunworth, Winslade, Woodgarston and Basingstoke. Basingstoke paid the most, 13s 4d every six months, and Somershill the least, on one payment of 6d in the autumn.

The officials of the Courts were the Steward, a Chairman, (a rich man of the district who does not seem to have been present at every court) two Bailiffs, elected two at a time to act for one year, (duties rather like magistrates) four Affeerors, who were to assess the amount of the fine to be paid if the Bailiffs imposed one (it had to vary with the offence and the status of the offender) and the jury of twelve or twenty-four men, who had to advise on custom, not guilt or innocence. Custom laid down what had always been done, the extent of each person's land, the common fields, who was the next heir, always relying on the memories of the men of the jury. The phrase was 'from time beyond which the memory of man does not go'.

The cases that came before the Bailiffs were most commonly ones of debt, then of damage caused to crops and land by men other than the occupant of the land. There were cases of assault, for fights were frequent, and of overcharging for goods or services. Beer brewed and sold below strength cost a fine, bread too light came up at every court. These Court Rolls tell us the names of people, their trades, the names of their houses and those of the

JUST TAPES

1 LONDON STREET
BASINGSTOKE

Tel: Hackwood 2231

FOR ALL THE LATEST VIDEO HIRE FILMS
by

Alan Sinclair

Alan Sinclair

★ COLOUR TV
★ VIDEO RECORDERS
★ HI-FI
★ AERIAL INSTALLATION
★ RADIO

Sales & Service
Video & Colour T.V. Rentals
9–11 CHURCH STREET
BASINGSTOKE
Tel: Basingstoke 21307

Top Market, on the site of the old Market Place is one of the oldest parts of the town. The Town Hall was built in 1832 and replaced the 1647 building which would have stood at the bottom left of this picture.

fields round the town.

Along high ground at the top of the town ran the road from London to Winchester. In the centre of the town, on this road, was the Market Place, and probably the Mote Hall or common meeting place of the town, where the courts were held. From the Market Place two roads ran downhill, one past the church named Church Street, and the other Ote Street. Ote Street descended to the river, crossed it by Coppid Bridge, turned east by Withgaresmead and climbed the hill on the way to Reading. Otherwise one went in the valley along Water Lane to Basing. Church Street crossed the river, perhaps by a bridge called Town Bridge, but there seems to have been a ford there too. There it became Chapel Hill, also called Whiteway or Holy Ghost Street, because it led to the Chapel of the Holy Ghost. After the chapel it would have passed the town rabbit warren at Park a Privet, then on to Sherborne and eventually to Newbury.

The road from London, after the Market Place, went west for a couple of hundred yards and one part turned sharply downhill towards Andover and Salisbury. The other part went to Winchester. Across the bottom of Church Street and Ote Street ran a street which was North Brook Street or Frog Lane, leading towards Worting on the west, past the part of the river used to wash sheep at shearing time.

Besides the roads there were hedges and ditches to keep animals out of the common fields, and to drain the water off the roads. It was a case for presenting at the three-weekly court if the man who had land by the ditch allowed it to become blocked so that the road was flooded, or let his hedge or gate fall down. It was not unusual for a man to dig a hole in the road by his house, either to get clay to plaster his walls or to make a saw-pit when he was building or repairing his house. The heavy beams were sawn as they were needed on the ground beside the house. From the list of fines for overcharging we find that there were carpenters, tilers and thatchers in Basingstoke, and some houses were roofed with shingles (short slabs of wood). It is unlikely that they had anything but a hole in the roof, no chimney, and there was no window-glass, just shutters to keep the wind out of the house.

When it came to furnishing the house there were joiners who could make chests and chairs. The chest was a very useful piece of furniture and could be for storage of clothes, blankets, flour, money or table linen and anything else that needed to be safe from thieves, damp or rats. It could also act as a working surface, a seat or a bed. The bedstead was merely a rectangular box to hold a straw, flock or feather mattress.

Basingstoke had butchers, fishmongers and bakers, so we know that at least they had meat and fish to eat as well as bread and beer,

SQUIRREL COLLECTORS CENTRE

ANTIQUE AND MODERN JEWELLERY

Antique Silver and
Collectables

9A New Street, Basingstoke
Hants. Tel: Basingstoke (0256) 464885

milk and butter and cheese. The bread was of different grades, the finest being simenell, with bran removed so it was the whitest bread, cokett (less fine), integer or mixed grain and the coarsest was horse-bread, a bran loaf hard and dry like dog-biscuit. A loaf that cost a farthing (¼ of an old penny) should have weighed 3½ pounds. Beer could be about ½d a gallon, but at that price it was not very strong.

The millers who ground the grain for the flour ran at least three mills, or maybe some of the mills were for fulling or cleaning grease from the cloth that had been woven by the weavers in the town. Basingstoke also had tailors, tanners, shoemakers, candle-makers, smiths, braziers who made copper and brass pots, haberdashers selling linen cloth, belts and girdles, hosiers selling the long hose or stockings that men wore and coopers making and selling tubs and wooden buckets and barrels.

If a man who was ordered to pay a fine either refused to pay or had no money, then his goods were taken and sold until the fine was made up. The tithing man or any suitable neighbour just went into his house and legally removed the property. But it was a different matter when the miscreant was somebody of the rank of knight, and it happened that Sir John Wallop took advantage of this difficulty when he wanted to run his 700 sheep on Basingstoke Down, where he had no business to be, and his servants cut down thorn bushes and scattered them all over the Down so that the cattle who had a right to be there could not get at the pasture. About two years before, he had been fined £10 and does not seem to have paid his fine.

In normal times the bailiffs or steward would have appealed to the king. But the Wars of the Roses began in 1459 and these minor local matters would not have been dealt with. It is more than probable that Sir John was confident that he would not be commanded by the king to pay the fine. Sir John was obviously one of the new farmers who concentrated all their efforts on producing the wool that could be sold for such a high price abroad. Sheep need fewer men to look after them, so there began to be unemployment in many agricultural areas.

Because of this trouble with Sir John, the men of Basingstoke wrote down the regulations for the organisation of the fields. They said, very firmly, that no tenant living outside the town (Sir John lived at Farleigh) was to occupy the common with his cattle and no

Bailiff was to let the land to him. If they had taken money from him as rent they were to pay twice the amount they received from him to the Church.

They gave the duties of the shepherd, the swineherd and the hayward. The shepherd was to be sure the sheep in his care did not stray into the crops, and he had to pay a fine to the owner of the crop if it was damaged. The same applied to the swineherd and the pigs he was to watch. The hayward looked after the hedges, not hay, and he was to put straying animals in an enclosure called a pound, where the owner had to pay a fine before the stray was allowed out. There was one pound up near the Holy Ghost Liten and another along Winchester Road.

By 1464 the fields were Westfield, Nordern Field and Southfield (or Winchester Field). The Down was at the western end of Winchester Field. The three fields were probably sown three-yearly in rotation, the first year spring sown, the next winter sown and the third left fallow. The Down was simply sheep pasture. Although the fields were almost certainly divided into strips, there was no choice about the crop – the whole field had the same crop. In the open field system, one field had the wheat or rye sown in the

Turnergraphic

DESIGN · TYPESETTING · PRINT

LEADERS IN INFORMATION TECHNOLOGY

We can capture keystrokes from your computer/floppy discs via Compugraphic MCS Systems. Plus graphic design, paste-up and print all in-house.

Ring Dennis McCarthy

THE TOTAL PRINT SERVICE

Turnergraphic Ltd.,
Communications House, Alencon Link, Basingstoke, Hants RG21 1FN.
**Telephone (0256) 59252   Telex 858164 TURNER
Plus MODEM Text Transmission (0256) 28727
and Facsimile Transmission (0256) 51501**

St Michael's Church. The oldest part of the church is the small building at the east end with a Tudor chimney.

autumn (the winter field), while another had barley, oats or peas sown in the spring. The fallow field, uncultivated, rested but was probably grazed by the flocks of sheep and the cows, horses and pigs, so that it was trodden and dunged before it was ploughed again.

At harvest time the men must have known the limits of their own strips, though there were some mistakes occasionally. They were reminded in the regulations for the field not to drive their carts over another man's ground, and not to let pigs loose. Pigs not only rooted up crops but broke down hedges and got in the way of carts. When the whole field had been cut and carried home, then the animals were allowed in, but not until the gleaners had had their turn. Gleaners were poor people, either too old or too feeble to be able to earn money working at the actual harvest, but allowed to pick up loose ears of corn for their own use.

Barley was malted and beer made, which would not have been quite the same as beer today. There were no hops put in it, and because it was drunk very fresh, it was quite sweet. But at least it had to be made with boiling water poured onto the malt, so the dubious state of the water from the common river did not matter so much, as nobody drank it. Even children had beer, small beer, very weak.

Wheat, rye, oats and barley all made bread and porridge and thick soup. A poor man could have lived on bread and beer, though let us hope he would not have to, for, unless he was completely without relations, the family cared for their own old and infirm men and women.

Basingstoke in the fifteenth century was an almost self-sufficient community. They grew their own food, made provision for the poor who could not work, and had taken over the running of their own town.

The Tudor Period

At the beginning of the 16th century, several factors combined to quicken the pace of social and economic change in England. The influx of bullion from the New World caused widespread inflation, while the expanding profitable wool trade encouraged landowners to change from traditional arable husbandry to sheep farming.

The resulting rising prices and unemployment hit the agricultural labourers hardest, and there was bitter resentment by those disinherited during the enclosure movement towards the new capitalist landowners and 'the sheep that ate up men'. The disappearance of the traditional charitable agencies with the Dissolution of the Monasteries further worsened the situation of the poorer members of the country.

There were a variety of responses at national and local level to the related problems of poverty and public order caused by the threat of increasing numbers of sturdy beggars and the plight of those unable to support themselves.

As elsewhere, Basingstoke sought to impose limits on its obligations towards the poor. Here, each Hundred was to be responsible for housing and feeding its own paupers, and any person from outside the district was to be sent back to their place of birth or at least to the last place where they had lived continuously for three years. (Three years was known as legal residence). Sturdy beggars were discouraged by threat of imprisonment or by being put in the stocks for three days, or whipped through the town.

Basingstoke had its stocks near the Mote Hall in the Market Place. It also had its share of disorderly people to fill them. There was an innkeeper, living near the Market Square, who was notorious for lodging beggars, for allowing apprentices and servants to stay drinking and playing games till far too late at night. Apprentices were to be out of his house by 8 o'clock at night and servants by 9, the Bailiffs decided. He would be fined 40d a time if he lodged beggars for more than a night and a day. Games such as backgammon and cards and dice were not to be played except at Christmas time (even bowls and tennis were illegal in the Act of 1495). Apprentices and servants were not allowed to carry the long knives called basilards but of course everyone carried a knife of some sort to cut up their food. When a guest came to dinner he only expected to be supplied with a spoon, which could be wood, horn, pewter or silver.

The records of the town courts began to be partly in English. Formerly they had been written in the Latin that every educated man could understand. Now they had a section contributed by the tithingmen and the more solid citzens, with complaints about the prices of bread and beer, the state of the ditches and roads, and the bad behaviour of men like Pether who kept the riotous alehouse.

The fines imposed by the Courts seem very small until it is realised how small the wages were. A national regulation of 1514 laid down that a freemason, carpenter, rough mason, bricklayer, master tiler, plumber, glazier or joiner was to be paid 6d a day during the summer months, from Easter to Michaelmas. If he was given food he was only to get 4d daily. For the rest of the year he was paid 5d a day, 3d with food. Every other labourer could earn 4d a day in the summer without food, 2d if fed. At harvest time the wages went up to 6d a day without food, 4d with. A woman got 4½d

W.W. HALL LTD
Building Material Distributors

For... Building Materials

★ Large stocks of Building & Patio materials
★ Friendly & helpful advice
★ Kitchen & Bathroom Display
★ Crane Off-Load vehicles available
★ Tel: (0256) 473251

W.W. HIRE
TOOL & EQUIPMENT HIRE

For... Tool & Equipment Hire

☆ Comprehensive range of Tools & Equipment
☆ Trade & Retail welcome
☆ Long & short term hire
☆ Delivery service
☆ Tel: (0256) 54025

Rankine Rd, Daneshill West Ind. Est., Basingstoke
Open Mon–Fri 7.30–5.00 Sat 7.30–12.00 noon

Church Cottage, one of the oldest buildings in the town, is mainly Tudor.

a day without food. So it seems that it was possible to feed a grown person for 2d a day.

They worked very long hours, in summertime beginning before 5 in the morning and not finishing until 7 or 8 in the evening. They were allowed half an hour for breakfast and one hour for dinner, except in the heat of the summer, from mid-May till mid-August, when they could take half an hour extra for a sleep. In winter, work began at first light and went on until dark.

Tailors, weavers, joiners and shopkeepers were fined from 3d-4d for overcharging and labourers 2d, so they had to pay half a day's wages for their misdoings. The men who earned more, the millers and inn-keepers, could be fined as much as 3s4d if they were brought to court.

From the records of the courts and from the wills that can be read, it is known that there were several shops in Basingstoke. There were butchers and bakers, mercers who sold a fine mixture of goods, paper, cotton and linen cloth, spices, drugs, oils and salves, tape and ribbon and pins, even ready-made shirts and straw hats. There were shops selling nothing but woollen cloth, a shop for knives and daggers, one for leather goods and a shoe-shop. There were at least two smiths, one in the Market Square and another along London Street.

The main industry was the growth and treatment of sheep and wool. A live sheep could produce wool yearly, and an ewe could be milked. Dead, there was mutton and lamb, fat for candles and rush-lights and skin for parchment The sheep were washed and sheared in the field called Sheepwash Meadow, where the river ran. It can still be seen as a tiny trickle going through the green patch west of Victory Roundabout, and the green is all that is left of the Sheepwash Meadow. Wool is easier to spin and weave with the natural grease still in it, but the filaments must be straight before they can be spun, so they were combed or carded before being spun into thread on the wheels that seem to have been in nearly every kitchen in Basingstoke.

Carding and spinning were woman's work, but weaving had become a job for a man. Some houses had looms and racks to stretch the woven cloth. After weaving, the cloth was fulled, (cleaned from the grease by having fullers earth rubbed into it and then washing the cloth). At first, the fuller trod the earth into the wool with his feet, but later mills were fitted with big padded hammers, raised by water-wheels. The records do not say which of the three mills was for fulling, but we know where one fuller lived. He had a house at the bottom of the lane later called Bunnian Place. (Somewhere under the present Civil Service Commission building off the Alencon Link). His name was Richard Kingsmill, and because there was another, richer, Richard Kingsmill he was always referred to as Richard Kingsmill, fuller. The grander Kingsmill owned most of the houses on the south part of Winchester

A Fantastic Selection of Glassware!

We offer a wide selection of lead crystal, party glass, kitchenware and vases.
Also hundreds of items including seconds and discontinued lines at bargain prices.

WESTERN GLASS INTERNATIONAL
Armstrong Road, Daneshill East.
Basingstoke, Hampshire.
Tel: (0256)462341

ACCESS AND BARCLAYCARD WELCOME

Shop Hours
Mon,Tues,Wed,Thurs,Fri 10a.m.~5p.m.
Sat 9a.m.~2p.m.

Street in 1509 when Katharine of Aragon stayed in his house on her way to Dogmersfield.

The names of the houses and the rent paid for them can be found by reading the Rentals from the town. Each house-owner paid a Quit Rent every six months, and this was an important part of the income of the town. The 'quit' meant that the money was instead of the duties that the lord of the manor used to demand. The names of the families and the names of their houses, can also be found for of course they were not numbered. Most of the house-names came from the first owner, so that Russell's house was just Russells, Edmund Tauk gave his name to Tawkes, Valans to Vallances. We are told what was inside these houses from the inventory that had to be taken when a man died, so that he could be taxed on the value before the will was proved and the relations got their legacies.

Each will begins with a commendation of the soul to 'all the company of heaven, and my body to the earth from whence it came' and leaves money to the parish church and to the church in Winchester (St Swithin's cathedral). In the earlier years of the century, men and women left money to be spent on masses for their souls, but in 1529 there was an Act forbidding any spiritual person to take any money to sing for any soul. Henry VIII had begun his campaign to take over the enormous income of the Church. He had almost spent the money his father Henry VII had so carefully amassed, and by 1535 he had managed to get tithes of all ecclesiastical benefices assigned to him.

Lord Sandys had a chapel built on the south side of the Chapel of the Holy Ghost where he meant himself and his family to be buried. By the year this was built, 1524, the whole chapel was famous for fine paintings in the roof, wonderful glass in the windows, and a statue of the Holy Spirit. There was an attempt to tax the chapel for tithe because it was thought to be a chantry, where money had been left to pray for the soul of the benefactor. But the Gild of the Holy Ghost managed to establish that the income was only to pay the chaplain, not for prayers for the donor. The money in question was only a tenth of £6:13:4, so it was hardly worth the king bothering to get 13s4d.

But if he was merciful, his son Edward VI was not. Edward had an uncompromising attitude to religion, he disliked all superstition and errors in Christian religion, he did not believe in purgatory or masses for the dead, and in 1547 chapels set up to sing masses for

Sainsbury's and Basingstoke have grown up together.

Back in 1964 our first "out-of-town" depot was opened in Basingstoke, in the Houndmills Estate.

Four years later the first Sainsbury's store in the area opened.

It proved so popular, we closed it. Replacing it instead with one and then another of our newest, biggest and most up-to-date stores. Sainsbury's depot became even more important, and today it employs more than 1,500 local people.

Add all this to our new Homebase house and garden centre in the town and one thing's for sure.

Basingstoke wouldn't be the same without us.

Sainsbury's

2 Station Mall	Brightonhill Parade
The Basingstoke Centre	Brighton Hill
Basingstoke	Basingstoke

Winchester Road, Basingstoke

An iron chest intended to hold deeds and valuables, thought to have been the property of the Gild of the Holy Ghost.

the soul of one person, and small foundations like the Holy Ghost Chapel were dissolved. The funds were lost too, now payable to the Crown. The inhabitants of Basingstoke only had to wait until 1556, when Queen Mary was on the throne and married to Philip of Spain. After a petition to Philip and Mary, supported by Cardinal Pole, the Archbishop of Canterbury, the Chapel, the Gild and presumably the funds were restored.

The Accounts of the Gild, begun in 1558, tell us about the expenses of the school for the repair of the buildings and the work done making desks and places to hang the scholars caps. The schoolmaster was paid £12 a year in 1559.

A casualty of the Dissolution of the Monasteries was the image in the chapel, the one of the Holy Spirit, slightingly referred to as 'that painted post' so it must have been of wood. It was demanded by the king's officers and sent up to London to be burnt.

St Michael's Church in the town had altars to different saints, and must have had images as well, but there is no record that they were taken away. Before all the trouble over prayers for the dead, people asked in their wills for candles to be lit for them before the altar they were particularly devoted to. There was the high altar, to St Michael, while at the east end of the nave was the Jesus altar, or Rood altar. At the east end of the north aisle was one to St Mary and on the other side of the church one to St Thomas. There was also a chapel to St Stephen.

The church had at least one bell, which may have rung to wake the men in time to go to work in the mornings, as well as for a knell. Alderman Ronegar left money to buy a bell to be hung in the church, which may be one of the oldest bells, dedicated to St Margaret. One of his daughters was named Margaret.

There were some seats in church, for several people asked to be buried at their seats end. One of the shops in the town sold matins books, so some of them could read well enough to follow a service, and a few could write, as the Court Rolls in English show. However, very few Wills are signed with anything more than a mark.

They may have begun to be better educated, but they knew very little about disease. They imagined that a bad smell produced illness, and the gaol fever (typhus) spread by lice and dirt, was counteracted by a pleasant smelling bunch of herbs. Of course, even if for the wrong reasons, it was sensible to ask the butchers not to let all the mess of the slaughter-house run out into the street, and to tell the fishmongers to clean up their fish-boards and not to let them stand in the market all night. Tanners and dyers were forbidden on pain of a fine, to let the dirty water from the tanning and dyeing out of the vats into the river before sunset or after sunrise. This gave the river time to wash away the smelly liquids before anyone wanted to get water out for cooking and washing.

Throughout the Tudor period the poor were dealt with in various ways, none of them providing satisfactory solutions. Finally in 1601 the Poor Law Act set down the responsibilities for each parish to provide for their poor. Overseers of the Poor were to be appointed, to include the Churchwardens and up to four substantial house-holders. Their duties were to maintain the poor and set them to work, men usually to work on the roads and women to spin, knit or plait straw. The money for the maintainance was to be provided by taxation of every inhabitant. Houses of Correction were to be built. Basingstoke had at least one, site unknown, and four Overseers of the Poor yearly.

There was no Workhouse at this time, the poor were to be cared for by their own families if possible, or a neighbour was paid as a nurse or foster-mother. Indeed, for the next century all poor persons brought their petitions for relief before the town court, the court made an order and the Overseers carried it out. If he did not get his money, the pauper could appeal and the overseer was compelled to pay his pension. As well as sums of money, which were generally sixpence or a shilling a week, help was given in payment for repairs and building to the houses of the poor, clothes were bought, medicines and doctors paid for, and children apprenticed.

From the accounts of the Overseers of the Poor we find that there was at least one doctor in the town, Doctor Crompton. Other unqualified men and women were paid for 'cures' and for bleeding patients. There was also an apothecary with a very well stocked shop, who kept three books in his shop, herbals and dispensatories, so he could have advised on medicines as well.

The Seventeenth Century

At the beginning of the 17th century, it became fashionable to leave money in wills for charitable purposes. Sir James Deane left money in 1607, to set up Almshouses. Mathew Stocker left 10s p.a. to the poor in 1619, George Pemberton left £5 p.a. for the same use in 1634. Sir James Lancaster left a great deal of money to be invested and the income to the poor, to school-teachers and a lecturer. Richard Aldworth in 1646 gave £2,000 to buy land which would give an income of £103:10:8 to set up a school, to pay a lecturer, and a sum to be given to the master of every boy apprenticed from the school. John Wigg left money for a yearly payment to the master of the Grammar School and to the poor. John Smith gave £4 annually so that clothes could be made for eight poor people every year. Sir James Deane and Richard Aldworth also donated money for bread to be given weekly to poor people of the town, and Richard Aldworth hoped there would be enough money left to give gowns to ten old men and women. Sir James Deane's Almshouse in London Street is still there and has quite lately had some improvements which are not visible from the street. Richard Aldworth's School was in Cross Street.

By the middle of the century, there were three schools for boys, the Free School, a school concentrating on Greek and Latin Grammar, the Aldworth School (Blue-coat School) which educated boys from 7-16 and then arranged for an apprenticeship for them, and a Petty School teaching children to read and write. The Grammar school would not take a boy until he could read. All these schools were all for boys, it does not seem that girls were provided with any formal education at all.

In 1622 the town of Basingstoke had obtained another charter. Instead of the 'proved men' of the town there were to be Bailiffs and Burgesses. Burgesses were the upper class of men of the town, responsible and well-off. Out of them were to be chosen 14 of the best and most upright who were to be called Capital Burgesses, who were to be a Council and to assist the Bailiffs. These Bailiffs were elected from the Burgesses yearly. The first High Steward was the Marquess of Winchester and the under steward was John

Foyle Esquire. They now had two Officers called Serjeants at Mace who were to attend on the Bailiffs and carry silver and gilt maces. The Justices of the Peace were to hold a court every Tuesday. There could be a market every Wednesday and two fairs a year. The Bailiffs were to have a prison for safe custody, but they could only determine complaints about contracts, deceptions etc under the value of £10, and they could not try cases of murder or treason.

In 1639 the army of Charles I was defeated in his disastrous campaign against the Scottish Covenanters, and the King faced with bankruptcy. This increased his willingness to sell various exemptions and privileges. Thus in 1641, Basingstoke acquired another new charter, this time being granted a Mayor, Alderman and Burgesses, who were to form the Common Council of the town.

It was these same financial straits which forced Charles I to summon a meeting of Parliament that was ultimately to lead to open conflict between King and Parliament - the Civil War.

Deane's Almshouses viewed from the corner of New Road.

The decisive victory of the New Model Army at Naseby turned the tide of events in Parliament's favour, and as the war degenerated into a series of sieges of Royalist strongholds Basingstoke was thrust (albeit unwillingly) into the forefront of events. The town was no longer able to continue in a non-partisan attitude. While already reluctantly providing £40 per week to supply the garrison of Basing House, they also were providing cloth and food for the Parliamentary army which laid siege to it.

Because of the strategic importance of Basing House, the Parliamentary forces made a determined effort to reduce it. The eventual defeat of the garrison at Basing House under the Marquess of Winchester in October 1645 was to be an important factor in the concluding stages of the war. Probably many Royalist fortresses were induced to surrender without prolonged resistance by the fate of Basing House. After its successful storm Cromwell wrote 'We have had little loss: most of the enemy of our men put to the sword, and some officers of quality; most of the rest we have prisoners'.

During the battles, soldiers were buried in the churchyard at Basingstoke. The church was damaged both outside and inside, the

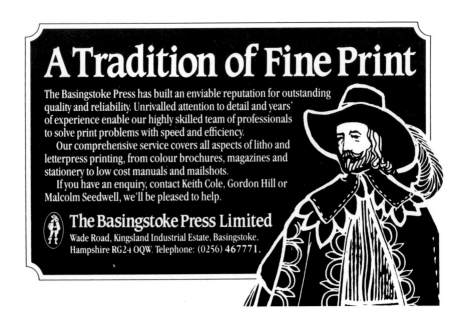

A Tradition of Fine Print

The Basingstoke Press has built an enviable reputation for outstanding quality and reliability. Unrivalled attention to detail and years' of experience enable our highly skilled team of professionals to solve print problems with speed and efficiency.

Our comprehensive service covers all aspects of litho and letterpress printing, from colour brochures, magazines and stationery to low cost manuals and mailshots.

If you have an enquiry, contact Keith Cole, Gordon Hill or Malcolm Seedwell, we'll be pleased to help.

The Basingstoke Press Limited
Wade Road, Kingsland Industrial Estate, Basingstoke, Hampshire RG24 0QW. Telephone: (0256) 467771.

The storming of Basing House by Oliver Cromwell and the New Model Army, during the Civil War.

outer walls especially the south were pitted with shot-holes. The incident that caused them is not recorded. The inside damage was due to the explosion of barrels of gunpowder stored in the church. They had been stored in the south aisle, and all the glass on that side was blown out, even the clerestory windows high above. In 1646 the parish clerk had to go to Odiham to try to recover the Communion cup taken by Parliamentary soldiers in 1645.

After its surrender, the people who lived near Basing House were allowed to take away stone and tiles, and there is an entry in the records of the parish church of St Michael that some tiles from Basing were used to repair the roof of the chancel.

In 1657 the Market House was rebuilt after one of the bad fires that tended to afflict the town. Some of the houses in the town might still have been thatched, which would have increased the fire risk. The account, made by Mr Reve, listed the payments that were made for materials and labour, so that the progress of the work can be followed from the payment for the land on which the new Market House was to be built, from the cutting down of the trees, digging a saw-pit, to the actual sawing. Men got between 1s6d and 2s a day for ordinary labouring and building. Meat and drink was supplied, and drink for the men who carted the wood, bricks and tiles.

The House had a large window in the front with a balcony from which important announcements could be made. The building stood on twelve pillars, so that the space underneath could have been used as a covered market. There was a little tower on the roof, with a bell. The main room was decorated with the Commonwealth arms and was furnished with tables, stools and one great chair. There were cushions of red bassel, a carpet costing 16s6d, a silver cup and a clock with weights. The weather-vane on the top of the bell-tower was gilded. It was a most superior building, worthy of a Mayor, Alderman and Burgesses.

Also in the year 1657, Basingstoke had a witchcraft trial, of one Goody Turner. 1657 is a little late for affairs of this sort, for justices had become sceptical of the claims of both accusers and defen-

OAKLEY COACHES
(M. W. JONES)
CONTRACT AND PRIVATE HIRE - SOCIAL & SPORTS CLUBS

12, 29, 41, 45, 53 SEATER COACHES

WORKSHOP
& BOOKING OFFICE
Beach Arms Service Station
Andover Road
Oakley
Basingstoke
Telephone: Basingstoke 780731
(Until 6.00 p.m.)

OFFICE:
55 St. Johns Piece
Oakley
Basingstoke
Hants RG21 7JQ
Telephone: Basingstoke 781564
(After 6.00 p.m.)

YOUR FRIENDLY LOCAL COACH OPERATOR

The stump of a figure is all that is left of an Annunciation after damage to the church in the Civil War.

dants, and a witch would no longer have been hanged or burnt. If condemned at all, the witch could have been transported.

She was accused, in two very emotional depositions before the Justices, of killing a little boy and bewitching a girl. The boy, named James Searle, aged eight, was going to play with the neighbour's children, but on the way he saw Joan Turner, and because he was afraid of her he turned aside to get over a stile. As he did so he felt a blow in his leg, and was not able to walk afterwards. He lay in bed becoming more feverish and died at the end of twenty weeks. (It is probable that he had osteomyelitis, which could have been due to infection when a brittle bone broke in his leg).

The girl had hysterical fits of some kind, and the case against Goody Turner was that she could calm the girl when no-one else could hold her. Finally, it was said that the child of Walter could not die until this Joan Turner came and said 'God release the child' – which seems rather out of character for a witch.

The next unpleasant event for Basingstoke was the appearance of the Plague in 1666. Mr Samuel Pepys of London had seen plague crosses on doors in June 1665. It was thought that the Plague came over from Dutch ports. In terror, people left London for the country. In September 1665 a man died of plague in Basingstoke. There was a lull during the winter, but in May 1666 three more men died. By August whole families had suffered. Forty-eight burials are marked in the Burial Register as being of the Plague, but more than seventy knells are said to have been rung. Cases were still recorded up to November of 1666, when the Plague subsided.

The case of Mrs Blunden, buried alive, was not only locally notorious, but a leaflet was published in London describing a version of the events. It took place in 1674, when Mrs Blunden, described as a gross woman, found herself suffering from a headache and sent for some poppy-water (a mild form of opium). She seems to have had a bad headache for she drank too much, sank into a deep sleep and eventually appeared dead. No pulse could be felt, no mist showed on a mirror held over her mouth. Although her husband, who was away, sent word not to bury her immediately, the weather was hot and thundery, and her household seem to have felt that she would not be in a very nice state if they waited until her husband came home, so she was buried in the Liten, near the boys' Free School.

The boys, coming to play, heard tappings and groans underground, but the Master did not believe them, and it was not until the next day that he was persuaded to listen himself and was convinced that they were not trying to deceive him. It was evening when she was got out of the ground, but by then she was definitely dead, and seemed to be badly bruised in her efforts to get out. She was left, with watchers, in case she revived, but during a storm in the night they ran away. By morning her grave-clothes were torn, they thought by herself, but more likely by foxes.

A coroner at her Inquest found that her life had been thrown away by over-hasty burying, but the evidence that a physician had used all the tests possible and *he* thought she was dead saved somebody being charged with murder.

Basingstoke again came into contact with the 'rude and licentious soldiery' in 1688, during the Glorious Revolution. William of Orange had landed at Torbay to take the crown and James II sent an army to oppose him, basing a large garrison at Salisbury. Sol-

News from
BASING-STOAK,
Of one
Mrs. BLUNDEN
A Maltſters VVife, who was
Buried Alive.

Relating how ſhe was over-heard by the
School-Boys, that were playing neer her
Grave, and afterwards by their *Maſter*, and
ſeveral others to repeat theſe words.

Take me out my Grave.

Whereupon ſhe was cauſed to be digged up, being found beaten
and bruſed in a lamentable manner; and all people then concluding her dead, they interred her again the ſecond time, but on the
morrow, which was five days after her Funeral, taking her up
again, they found ſhe had torn off her winding-ſheet, and beaten
her ſelf far worſe than before.

For which neglect ſeveral perſons were Indicted at the laſt Aſſizes
held at *VVincheſter*, and the Town of *Baſing-Stoak* compelled to
pay a great Fine.

Printed for *John Millet*.

A contemporary account of the death of Mrs Blunden published in London.

MARTIN AND STRATFORD

CHARTERED SURVEYORS, AUCTIONEERS & ESTATE AGENTS

Sales & Valuations for all purposes

13, CHURCH STREET, BASINGSTOKE

Telephone: Basingstoke 464141
also at
Alton, Andover, Winchester, and at
Avon & Wiltshire

ITT CANNON
the Basingstoke Connection

ITT Cannon have been designing and manufacturing electrical and electronic connectors since 1915 — providing a service to a wide variety of markets, from aerospace to telecommunications, from defence to business systems.

Just over 20 years ago, ITT Cannon moved from London to Basingstoke, since when it has become world leader in the connector field and one of the biggest employers in the area.

1983 saw the entire ITT Cannon Basingstoke operation being transferred to a new larger custom–built complex at the Viables Industrial Estate. This multi–million pound investment will enable further expansion and more job opportunities for the future.

Basingstoke & Cannon — growing together.

Cannon Electric (GB) Ltd
Jays Close
Viables Industrial Estate
Basingstoke RG22 4BW
Tel: Basingstoke (0256) 473171

diers on their way to or from there were obviously billeted at Basingstoke, for it is recorded that a Mrs Margaret Barwicke was robbed of £25, a black hood, a long scarf and a pair of purple shoes by two soldiers billeted upon her. (The same men were apparently in trouble again a week later at Whitchurch where they attacked a couple and extracted 27/6d from them).

This had been a turbulent century for Basingstoke. Thankfully, the soldiers who had caused so much annoyance to Mrs Barwicke would be the last to be billeted on the town for 226 years.

The Eighteenth Century

The Civil War, and other wars of the 17th century against France and Spain had swelled the numbers of the poor and unemployed, this time in the form of demobilised soldiers and sailors and the widows and orphans of those killed in action. Help for the destitute was extremely grudgingly administered, and the poor made to feel ashamed and guilty of their 'crime' of poverty.

In 1697 an Act of Parliament required that 'Every pauper and his wife and children shall wear upon his right shoulder of his uppermost garment a large Roman P together with the first letter of the Parish in red or blue cloth'. This was called the Badging of the Poor and is duly set down in the accounts of the Overseers of the Poor in Basingstoke for 1698 – 'For cutting the badges, 2s2d'.

In 1722 parish officers were authorised to buy or rent workhouses. Persons who declined to enter the workhouse to have no more relief. In Basingstoke, on October 10th 1726, ten people (six women, two children and two men) were ordered to the Workhouse. From the lists of things bought for the Workhouse we find that the inmates were given meat (beef and mutton at 3d-4d a pound), bread, and beer which they had to brew themselves. They grew vegetables in their garden. Mrs Edwards, the Matron was paid 12s a month. The women were supplied with spinning wheels. The Workhouse was in Brook Street, more or less where the Victory Roundabout is today.

Vagrants were still pursued and sent back to their place of last legal residence. One of them was called Ann Paice. She was discovered near Peterborough, questioned by a magistrate, and she confessed her place of birth was Basingstoke. She was sent back with a warrant to the constable of each place she had to pass through. She was sent off on January 18th 1711, and reached Basingstoke on the 2nd of February, travelling about ten miles a day. Vagrants were allowed 6d a day maintenance and were sometimes carried by cart, but she could have walked at that rate.

Although there was some income derived from charities, such as that of Sir James Lancaster, for the maintenance of the poor, the rest had to be supplied from the poor rate. It appears to have been the duty of the Justices of the Peace to decide what rate the parish should pay (not more than 6d a week) and by the rate in Basingstoke they raised a varying sum yearly, in 1679 it was £119·3·9d, in 1702 £214·3·10d. The Overseers of the Poor collected the money and paid it out as it was needed all round the year. A person who refused to pay the Rate had their goods taken and sold to raise the sum due. Quakers refused to pay, and so we know that there were at least five of them, Mr Applegarth, Dr Portsmouth, Thomas Hack, Richard Wallis and Sarah Mitchel. The Quaker Meeting House was in the house next to the Rose Inn at the bottom of Chapel Hill or perhaps actually in the Rose. Later they had a large house in Wote Street. Other non-conformists were the Congregationalists, who had a regular meeting house near the Blue-coat School in Cross Street from 1695.

Some Non-conformist meetings took place occasionally and rather stormily. John Wesley visited Basingstoke more than once and preached here, but he thought the people 'like wild beasts'.

In 1739 a Reverend Mr Charles Kinchin caused a lot of annoyance to the Vicar by holding a meeting of Dissenters in the Crown Inn in Basingstoke, where he is said to have prayed much *extempore* and taken a whole chapter for his text, the noted Mr Whitfield from Georgia preaching at the Kings Head on one day and at the Crown on the Friday and Saturday preceding. Mr Warton wanted him stopped, and he hoped that the magistrates could find some penalty, for the house was not licensed for religious worship, and Mr Kinchin had not declared himself a Dissenter. The Countess of Huntington established Dissenting chapels, hoping to appeal to well-to-do people and convert them to the chapel. She had chapels in places like Tunbridge Wells. Basingstoke must have been rather surprised to get one, and perhaps a little flattered. The Countess' chapel was in Wote Street, next to the site where Jukes the chemist now stands.

Travelling, all over England, was uncomfortable and sometimes dangerous, when either highwaymen robbed the coaches or the heavy vehicles got stuck in the deep pot-holes and mud in the roads which had no body responsible for their repair. A man complained of being robbed by a highwayman up near Park Prewit (called park privit then). He took forty shillings from him and rode off on a large black horse. Other cases of coaches being robbed came before Basingstoke Justices.

By 1784, when a Directory of Basingstoke was printed, there were coaches coming up from Salisbury, Exeter, Southampton, Bath and Bristol, through Basingstoke to London. They stopped at the George, the Wheatsheaf, the Three Tuns and the Feathers, while the Bath and Bristol coaches used the Crown. There was a coach to each of these places every day, going up to London in the evening, and the other way in the small hours of the morning. Wagons ran too, and seem to have gone from the Angel and the Anchor. The Inns are mostly still public houses, the Red Lion, the Feathers, the George and the Wheatsheaf are all to be found, but the Crown and the Angel have gone. The Crown was where Joices Yard is, the Angel a few doors west of the George. The Three Tuns probably went when Victoria Street was made. There were others, the Bell, the Black Boy (which is still with us but called the Hop-leaf), the Fleur-de-lys (now the main Post Office), the Bell (opposite the Fleur-de-lys), the Rose and the Rose and Crown which were demolished with other younger pubs in the 1960s.

Throughout the 18th century roads were being improved by the turnpike trusts. These consisted of local interested groups such as

THE VAUXHALL CENTRE

BASINGSTOKE   A GROWING TOWN

J. DAVY   A GROWING COMPANY

VAUXHALL   BETTER BY DESIGN

J. DAVY   BETTER BY FAR

BASINGSTOKE   J. DAVY   BASINGSTOKE
462551   WEST HAM, BASINGSTOKE   462551

The Old Angel Cafe, originally The Angel Inn.

landowners, merchants and professional men who undertook to put a particular stretch of road into good repair. Toll gates were then erected by the trust and traffic charged to travel along the improved road. There were toll gates in Basingstoke near the Toll House Kiosk in Hackwood Road, one near the Rising Sun on Chapel Hill, one along Worting Road by Greenway, one on Winchester Road by the Hare and Hounds and one down by Black Dam.

Miss Jane Austen the novelist used to pass through Basingstoke, perhaps on her way to Bath, and she also went to dances in the Assembly Room behind the Angel. In her book *Emma* there is a description of a dance that Emma went to which shows the kind of affair that might have been held in the Angel. Her mother's doctor, Mr Lyford, lived in Basingstoke and on one of her journeys prescribed her 12 drops of laudanum as a composer before bed. It seems as if she was a poor traveller.

Mr Lyford was not the only medical man in Basingstoke in the eighteenth century. In 1770 a Mr Covey was inoculating against smallpox. Smallpox was deadly, and many entries in the Church Burials register record 'died of the Pox'. He would have rubbed material from a smallpox blister into a cut on the arm of the victim, who stayed with him until the attack of smallpox was over. This was anything from 3 weeks to nearly six.

We can form a picture of the town of Basingstoke in 1762 from a map that was drawn in that year. It was to show the land owned by various landlords, but it was not the sort of map seen today. Not only were the strips of field shown with the name of the person who farmed it written along its length, but when the draughtsman thought a building was important he drew a little picture of that, too. There is a tiny Town Hall, the Rectory, the Church, the ruins of the Holy Ghost Chapel, some large houses and mills and barns. The River and the streams that join it wind about at the bottom of the town and all the closes behind the houses are shown with trees and hedges. Some of the meadows are named, Hogwash and Sheepwash and Longcroft along the stream that can still be seen trickling through the green patch where Brook Street used to be, to the west of Victory Roundabout.

HAYMARKET THEATRE

The Haymarket Theatre is the home of Basingstoke's own Professional repertory Company — The New Horseshoe Theatre Company.

ENJOY — the cream of the classics
— the most loved of popular revivals
— the pick of important contemporary work

The Haymarket also presents concerts, children's shows ballet, touring drama, large scale musicals and there are regular performances by Basingstoke's popular local amateur groups; it is truly a community theatre.

WOTE STREET. BASINGSTOKE. Box Office (0256) 465566   (0256) 477358

CENTRAL STUDIO

"MODERN THEATRE AT ITS VERY BEST"
BASINGSTOKE GAZETTE

FOR INFORMATION WRITE TO THE CENTRAL STUDIO, QUEEN MARY'S COLLEGE, CLIDDESDEN ROAD, BASINGSTOKE HANTS. RG21 3HF
FOR BOOKINGS TEL: BASINGSTOKE 465566

The Assembly Room behind the Angel Inn where Jane Austen once danced.

There are at least two buildings still standing that certainly date from the eighteenth century. One is the old Rectory (Chute House) and the other is Goldings in the Park by the Council Offices. The Rectory was rebuilt in 1758, so it was new when the map was made. Goldings is more elaborate for it included a timber framed building which was reconstructed about 1700. The room that became the Mayor's Parlour was panelled with pine and the open brick fireplace lined with Lambeth tiles. About 1780 it was enlarged and the main entrance in London Road closed, with a new entrance made on the east side. Until quite lately there was a feature called a ha-ha in the park (a concealed ditch to keep animals in open park land away from the front of the house).

The map was to be completely changed in 1786, when the common fields were all enclosed except for a common of 107 acres at the east end of the town. Tenants who had common rights were allowed to put cattle on it from May to January, their rights calculated at so much in the pound of the value of the property, and called 'legs on the common'. The total number of animals that the common could carry was 276, but it was said in 1880 that there were rarely more than 180. Land was allowed for a Fair at the end of Allens Lane (Victoria Street) because the Down had been taken, and there was half an acre for a chalk or gravel pit. Land was set aside to enlarge the Workhouse garden, and there was a place for a House for Infectious Diseases, the Pest House.

Although the roads were improving, transport of goods was still slow by waggon and delayed by bad weather winter and summer. Heavy goods, coal, lime, corn, pottery and bricks were more easily carried by water, even round the coast from Bristol to Kent. But dues had to be paid at ports, floods and strong winds could slow up

Joice's works occupied the old Crown Yard and the buildings round it. They were once part of the Crown, one of the coaching inns of the town.

the vessels, even pirates might have to be reckoned with. In 1758 the Duke of Bridgewater made an artificial river from Worsley to Manchester, so successful that the price of the coal he sent could be halved, and still be very profitable.

Canals were seen as the solution to many trading problems, and the Duke's engineer, James Brindley, was consulted with a view to joining Basingstoke to a canal that the town of Reading was proposing from Sonning to Monkey Island. Permission had to be got from Parliament, and there were objections to the Reading part of the canal. People were afraid that the Thames would silt up if it was not in constant use, and if a canal burst it might flood villages.

In 1778 Basingstoke tried again. A canal was said to be of great use in bringing good coal down from London, and taking grain and timber back. A complaint from Sir James Tylney that the canal would spoil his land caused the planners to propose to dig a tunnel through Greywell Hill to pacify him. The Royal Assent was given to the plans for the canal in 1778, with the limitations that no water was to be taken from the Lodden, so as not to injure the water-mills. There were eventually 29 locks and 72 bridges, all of which the Company had to keep in repair. The contract for the construction was given to John Pinkerton in 1788, the delay being due to the war with America. Investors, invited to buy bonds, were promised that an income of £8,000 could be expected from 30,000 tons of goods carried. Passage and pleasure boats cost 6d a lock.

The canal was opened in the autumn of 1794, and the next month the southern bank of the canal near the west end of Greywell Tunnel collapsed and clay blocked the canal. Traffic to Basingstoke had to stop till the end of the year, and in any case the ice was too thick for boats to get through in the winter. By 1796 the company was almost bankrupt, for the interest on the bonds had to be paid,

Curtis Carpets

SPECIALIST PLANNING, FITTING and ADAPTATIONS of CARPETS and VINYLS, CLEANING by HOT WATER EXTRACTION. Free Estimates. Domestic or Contract Distance No Object

Phone GARY HOPKINS on:-
BASINGSTOKE (0256) 59721

35 MILKINGPEN LANE, OLD BASING, BASINGSTOKE, HANTS.

but there had been no profits. Gradually changes were made in the Company and a small profit was made, £2,000 in 1801.

In 1812 part of the tunnel fell in and trade was lost while it was being repaired. There was not enough trade anyway, for the only other town on the canal was Odiham. If it had been possible to link Basingstoke to Southampton and Bristol, which was considered, then things would have been very much better, but the troubles that the Basingstoke Canal had suffered were only too evident, and nobody wanted to lose money in another scheme. The final blow came when the railway was opened to Basingstoke in 1839 and to Southampton in 1840; trade improved while it was being built, for the materials were carried on the Canal, but railways were faster, more progressive, reliable. Even Queen Victoria travelled by train. The Wharf at the bottom of Wote Street (the area where the garage, cinema and Bus Station are today) was put up for auction.

There was still some traffic in goods on the canal for a time. Pleasure parties, too, went on the canal for day-long picnics taking bands to play to them on the way. When there was a hard winter skaters could get to Basing or further, but the expense of keeping

PROBLEM with holidays, sickness and busy peak periods.

Our specialist temporary staff can help you overcome this. Thoroughly interviewed, referenced checked and skill measured, we can supply the following services:

OFFICE — TECHNICAL & SKILLED & INDUSTRIAL

Trust us to solve your problems.

Office hours: 8.00 a.m. – 5.30 p.m.

Hampstead House, New Town Centre, Basingstoke, RG21 1LG. Tel: (0256) 29629

the canal open was just too much. A timber yard took over the wharf and the water became green and stagnant. The line of the canal can still be followed along the hedge at south side of the Eastrop Park, one of its boundary hedges, and the big willow trees on the other side once hung over the water.

By the end of the 18th century, the coaching era and the building of the canal had brought about an improvement in communications not only in the physical movement of traffic, but in the traffic of different ideas and view points. Thus market towns such as Basingstoke were becoming less insular and more aware of wider horizons. This paved the way for the changes which were to come during the next century.

The Victorian Era

The 19th century brought many changes to the town from the introduction of the threshing machine and other agricultural innovations, to the beginnings of new industries for Basingstoke.

At the beginning of the century the ever present problems of poverty were dealt with by the Overseers of the Poor. They collected the poor rate, and paid it out to eligible poor people, inspected the poor in the Workhouse and also advised the magistrates as to the character of the claimants. For this they were paid £80 per year by the Vestry. The Vestry dealt with matters of parochial administration, and their reports provide a wide view of life in the town up to about 1834.

In 1811 the officials of the Vestry were considering building a small Prison with a dwelling house next to it. The original lock-up was two long dark cells under the Town Hall apparently made of wood, for once a prisoner got his sister to bring him a large knife, saying it was to cut up bread and cheese, and cut a hole in the wall, but he does not seem to have escaped. Obviously the dungeon was too small and not really secure by 1811. The new site was in New Street, where the first Police Station was eventually built in 1816. This is very early – the Metropolitan Force was not started until 1829. The Basingstoke Force became part of the County Force in 1889.

As well as the Police, there was a watchman, with a great coat and hat provided, and a salary of £15. His name was John Hacker, and he walked round the town with a lantern, calling out the approximate time and commenting on the weather. After 1823 four more persons did the watching, with 2s a week each for their trouble.

About 1817 Mr Samuel Attwood began to keep a diary. He intended to record the hours that he worked for his father at his trade of a tailor, but gradually there crept in notes of the weather, interesting events in Basingstoke or the country in general. Mr Attwood set down everything that interested him, the games of cricket he played, the steam coach passing through the town, the erection and final fate of the only windmill that was put up in

The Basingstoke Beadle.

Basingstoke, and all the marvellous new buildings that the town was getting, the new Town Hall in 1832, the Gas Works in 1834, the new Poor House in 1835 (this was on Basing Road, backing onto the railway, now demolished), the opening of the Southampton Railway in 1839, the Grammar School in Worting Road in 1855, all welcomed by processions, bands playing and bells ringing, even the Gas Works.

The christening of the Prince of Wales in 1842 called for an even greater celebration, so as well as the usual parades there was money given to the poor, and they also got Beef, Mutton, Flour and Plums.

When the railway came, the mails went by train rather than the mail-coach, and the new Postmaster was a printer, Mr Cottle, who had a works in Winchester Street, on the south side. The slot where the letters were put into the Office has been found and is in the Willis Museum. It was discovered still in the wall when re-building was started.

New buildings were welcomed, but the new threshing machines were not, at least, not by the labourers who felt threatened by them. 1830 saw 'riotous persons assembling in a disorderly manner breaking machines ... 200 special constables sworn in ... military sent for ... shops shut in the evening. A number of prisoners brought in and all the town in confusion'. This was Mr Attwood's comment on the Swing Riots but he does not seem very disturbed by the poor labourers. As far back as 1811 the Vestry had been concerned about the number of poor out of employment, and they resolved that every man in husbandry (agriculture) should be paid 12s a week. They agreed in October 1820 not to use threshing machines, but they could not stop the machines being made, nor

CHURCH STREET PET SUPPLIES

For all your pet requirements

10A CHURCH ST., BASINGSTOKE.
Tel: Basingstoke 28204

Basingstoke Station.

the farmers using them. Emigration of the poor was suggested, with assistance being offered by the Vestry, but there was not much enthusiasm from the poor, who probably saw emigration as a form of transportation, which was a punishment for so small a crime as stealing a watch (in 1846 a man was transported for life for this). If to be sent to the colonies was a punishment, who wanted to go voluntarily?

The *Basingstoke Gazette* of 1926 had two articles by Mr Woodman of Odiham who wrote about Basingstoke 70 years before. Both Mr Woodman and Mr Attwood note a fire in a barn in Back Lane (Southern Road) where there were vegetables drying to be sent out to the soldiers fighting the Russians in the Crimea. Later in that same year, 1856, there was dinner to celebrate peace with Russia. The dinner was given to the poor of Basingstoke and Eastrop, the enormous number of two thousand and sixty, said Mr Attwood, and £220 pounds was subscribed for the dinner which was set out in the Market Place and nearby streets .. the bells rang and the bands paraded.

In 1857 the first stone of the two new chapels in the cemetery (the Liten north of the town) were laid. The architecture did not give universal satisfaction. In 1864 a Mr Grey of Godalming observed that it was a scandal that on the constituting of a cemetery at Basingstoke the Holy Ghost Chapel had not been repaired and used as a cemetery chapel 'But it may still outlive its pretentious party-coloured neighbours which I am glad to see are fast becoming ruinated'. He would be very pleased to see that both chapels he disliked were in fact pulled down, while the ruins of the Holy Ghost Chapel are still there. The Lodge at the west gate of the cemetery is in the same style, so anyone can judge whether he was right.

Improvements took place in the Parish Church of St Michael, when in 1865 Dr Millard preached in a church that was for the first time lit up with gas and heated with hot water in pipes. Until then, the building was neither heated nor lit and services were held only during daylight. The services were conducted in the old style – the psalms were read in alternate verses and some of the congregation wore smocks. The church then had a big cluster of chestnut trees outside, and the town bands used to play under the trees as the congregation came out of church.

The houses of the 1860s were also lit by gas, but upstairs it was oil-lamps or candles. The water came from a pump in the yard and the closet was outside, too, and often far too near the pump. The subject of drains had come up before the Council, but apart from putting a drain to take the torrents of rain-water that rushed down New Street and Church Street, nothing was done for some years after this was completed in 1839. The work was paid for by the Pavement Commission, separate from the Town Council, and they found they had not enough money to do anything more than this drain and the lighting of the town. Finally they transferred their property to the Council and left them to get on with the work themselves in 1873.

By 1878 there was still discussion but no drains, and plenty of opposition ... 'Can nothing be done to reverse a decision so disastrous to smaller rate-payers?' 'Is there no spirit in this old town to agitate against this enormous outlay ere it be too late?' By October 1878 the contractors seem to have been ready to start. It must have caused an immense upheaval. However, this was just the *drains*.

Water supply came ten years later. The supply seems to have been from a reservoir at South View, which might be the one next to St Thomas's School grounds in Darlington Road, and it was filled with water from a well off Reading Road, pumped up by a steam pump. The reservoir was there in 1886, and the waterworks at West Ham was opened in 1906. The water, being filtered through chalk, is very hard, but pure, 'the purest that can be found' according to an analyst in 1920.

There was a report to the Borough Council in 1894 on the possibility of establishing an Electricity Undertaking, but there was no supply until 1914, and then it was Direct Current from a works in Brook Street. It was very gradually changed to A.C. but the centre of Basingstoke was on D.C. until 1960.

The 1840 Gazeteer stated that there were 12 daily, 3 Sunday and 2 infant schools in Basingstoke. The Free School (the school in the Holy Ghost Chapel) had a master appointed by the Crown and an usher (assistant master) by the Corporation. The school had 13 boys. The Richard Aldworth School (the Blue-coat School) was educating 9 boys, and the largest schools were those established by Dr Sheppard and his wife. Dr Sheppard was lately Vicar of Basingstoke. The school was called the National School and taught 100 boys and 100 girls, the girls' school is said to have been in Church Cottage. About 1850 there was a school on Sarum Hill called the British School, founded mainly by the Society of Friends, Mr R. Wallis, the Quaker being one of those concerned.

The Free school, before it moved to Worting Road, was quite small and the usher had a small set of apartments there. It was not entirely free, for the Master charged 15s a quarter to teach boys from the town and £1 a quarter for those from outside. Classics lessons were free, but history, geography, writing and arithmetic were not. The Master got his income from the rent of Down Farm and 100 acres of land, which should have been £100 yearly. But in 1844 it was said to be reduced to £90 because of low prices paid for farm produce. He had to pay the usher £30 a year and also to keep the farm buildings in repair.

The Blue-coat School was rebuilt in 1862, by then it had united with the National Schools, and it appears that they were taught on the monitor system, where the master divided the pupils into groups of ten children, one of them being the monitor. He taught the monitors and they went back and taught the rest of the group.

The Blue-coat children learnt reading, writing from engraved copies, and arithmetic 'up to the Rule of Three'. This is a method of finding a fourth number if the other three are given i.e. 3 is to 4 as 6 is to? (8)

The other method of teaching large numbers of children with only one master was to use pupil-teachers. These were boys and girls who were apprenticed to the teachers, who got an allowance for teaching them. They had a five year apprenticeship from 13 years old until 18, and then sat an examination for a Queens Scholarship, which took them to a training college for three more years, after this they had a certificate. After 1884 pupil-teachers need not teach for more than half their time and the rest could be spent in training centres.

When St John's School was established in 1901, they had pupil-teachers, and the centre was Brook House for the girls, and possibly the Grammar School (the Free School or Queens School) for the boys. The first pupil-teacher in St John's was Reginald J. Figgis, who gained a Kings Scholarship in 1905 and had a salary of £65 a year.

Fairfields School was formed by amalgamating the British School and the National Schools in 1888. This was a Board School in contrast to St John's, which was an endowed school. It had been started by the Vicar of Basingstoke, the Reverend Dr Cooper Smith, and it had several managers, of which he was the Chairman. The Board Schools had a board of elected members, who had a term of three years. The Fairfields school was originally fee-paying, from 6d to 2d a week, depending on the wages of the parents and the number of children from the same family at school. The fees did not cover the cost, which was helped out by Government grants. These grants depended on the regular attendance of the pupils and the standard of education that they reached. Consequently there had to be inducements to the children to keep on coming to school. St John's gave half-holidays for good attendance of the whole school and Fairfields presented medals. These prizes were so effective that one boy got a watch for missing not one day out of seven years at school.

Classes were very large, even the babies class had 68 pupils when it began at St John's. The older boys went over to Sarum Hill to woodwork classes and the girls had cookery classes there. When it was very hot, they were allowed to go into the Rectory Garden and

A 19th century billhead showing some rather elegant customers.

do needlework under the trees, or quiet reading. If more than one member of staff was ill, the Headmaster was forced to take 100 children himself. This over-working probably contributed to the illness of the first Headmaster of St John's who was ordered to Folkstone after an attack of influenza in 1912 and died of consumption the following April. The average number for a class in Fairfields Boys school was 63 in 1888.

Even before the Industrial Revolution there had been some industry in the town. There was work in the Foundry of Wallis and Haslam, or on the Railway, or in May's Brewery. A traveller in 1722 noticed that Basingstoke had begun to enlarge its 'exports' by making druggets and shalloons. Druggets are felted coarse woollen fabrics, used as cheap carpets and shalloons are light woollen stuff, suitable for coat-linings. By the time the 1840 Gazeteer was describing the trade of Basingstoke, the manufacture of these woollen goods had declined, and that of malting increased. The most famous name in the malting and brewing business in Basingstoke was May. The two brothers Thomas and Charles May began with a large Malthouse in Brook Street, on the corner oppo-

Caledon & Butler

Estate Agents & Valuers

A Limited Company

A wide range of properties in the Basingstoke area always available

Extensive applicant register with literally hundreds of purchasers urgently seeking property within 15 miles of Basingstoke

Free valuations. No Sale — No Fee

Colour video service on all our properties

Residential Office:	1, Queens Parade, New St., Basingstoke, Hants. RG21 1DA Tel: Basingstoke (2056) 461322
Mortgage Office:	Rear Suite, 1 Queens Parade, New Street, Basingstoke, Hants, Tel: Basingstoke (0256) 59474
Accounts Office:	188 Aldershot Road, Church Crookham, Aldershot, Hants. GU13 0EW.

Chapel Street in the 1890s.

site the Rectory, and gradually bought alehouses and more buildings for the brewing of beer. Thomas lived in the Brewery House and Charles in Brook House, and they owned a farm in Brook Street, too, next to the Brewery.

By 1860, there were so many men employed at the Brewery and the Foundry not so very far away on Station Hill, that there needed to be more houses built suitable for the workers. There was so much opposition to the increase in housing that a proposed Railway Works went to Bishopstoke (Eastleigh) instead of to Basingstoke. But small houses were built, between the railway line and Worting Road, later called Newtown.

The foundry began as a small iron-foundry owned by Moses Caston on the south side of the Market Place, behind the shop later known to us as Kingdons, where the remains of the foundry could be seen in the 1960s. Richard Wallis joined Caston, and later a foundry was established in a strategic position near the Canal Wharf. While the canal still did business, coal and iron could be

You can always be sure of the quality and reliability of Sony Broadcast professional television equipment.

Products include:
- The Betacam Range
- Lightweight colour cameras
- ¾ inch U-matic Video Recorders
- 1 inch C format Video Recorders
- Electronic Editing Systems

- Digital Time Base Correctors
- Time Code Generators/Readers
- 1 inch, ¾ and ½ inch Video Tapes
- Monitors
- Professional Audio Equipment.

Contact your local
Sony Distributor
or write to

SONY ®
Broadcast

Sony Broadcast Ltd.
City Wall House
Basing View, Basingstoke
Hampshire RG21 2LA
United Kingdom

Telephone (0256) 55 0 11
International +44 256 55 0 11
Telex 85 84 24
Fax G2/G3 (0256) 47 45 85

delivered at the Wharf for the use of the foundry. Wallis and Sons became Wallis and Haslam, and finally Wallis and Steevens, a large works at the bottom of Station Hill. Richard Wallis and Sons cast animal feeding troughs, but they sold ploughs, harrows and rollers made by other firms. They also sold horse-powered threshing machines, which were almost obsolete by 1860, although small farmers liked them. A big steam-powered thresher with a team to work it went from farm to farm, and the bad-weather job of threshing with a flail was lost.

There were new industries which had their origins in Basingstoke. The first was Milwards, which was begun by Alfred Milward when in 1857 he opened a boot and shoe business in the town.

He lived in a tiny cottage and hawked shoes from a barrow, calling on clergy, gentry and inhabitants of Basingstoke and its vicinity. He had stocks of boots and shoes from some of the largest wholesale shoe houses in England. His first shop was in Winchester Street in Basingstoke. In 1890 he opened a branch in Broad Street in Reading, and eight years later the business became a limited company. (In 1903 the average price of a pair of sturdy mens boots was 6s11d).

Another well–known firm which began life in the town was that of Burberry coats. Mr Burberry is said to have noticed that the clothes of shepherds did not get soaked with rain, and he deduced that it was something to do with the grease from the sheep's wool. He made overcoats that shed rain instead of absorbing it and they were so popular that the overcoats took his name and became Burberries. He took on the shop at the end of Winchester Street on the site that was later to become Lanhams. Burberry's was the scene of a great fire on April 17th 1905. Some people in town may even still possess one of the souvenir mugs which were issued at the time.

It would be difficult to talk about the Victorian history of Basingstoke without mentioning Colonel John May. He was one of the Mays who owned the Brewery at the lower end of Chapel Hill, with the Brewery House next to Chapel Hill and the brewery buildings stretching out to the west along Brook Street, ending with Glebe Farm, also May property.

John May was born in 1837 and went to Queen Mary's School. He grew up to be an enthusiastic cricketer, keen on hunting (he kept harriers at the farm by the brewery). He became a J.P. and later a Mayor of Basingstoke, after serving the town as a member of the Town Council and as an Alderman.

Basingstoke benefited from his generosity and public spirit greatly, including a clock tower for the Town Hall, a new wing for the cottage hospital and the cricket ground of Mays Bounty, which is still there today.

His clock tower and another of his memorials are gone, however. His other memorial was the lamp standard in the Market Place, which he had decorated by adding a block of granite to it in Coronation Year October 1st, 1903. This bore four bronze plates. (1) a likeness of Colonel May   (2) a list of his mayoralties   (3) a list of the Mayoralties of his ancestors   (4) *one line* to say it was a Coronation memorial.

Mr George Willis would have made a very good Victorian of a different kind. He was born in 1878, educated at Fairfields School and went to Queen Mary's School with an Aldworth scholarship. He was top in both the religious and the secular sides of the scholarship examination. He became an historian and an archaeologist, and a keen botanist. As a boy, he found worked flints and fossils

HILSEA COLLEGE

Hilsea College is a splendid old country house
built about 1780, set in 300 acres of parkland,
5 miles west of Basingstoke

Founder: J. ELLIS–JONES, B.Sc. (Lond), L.C.P.

Day and Boarding College for Boys and Girls
from 5 to 16 years of age
Established 1914

Centre for GCE 'O' Levels (Oxford Board)

Principals
LANDON F. PLATT, B.A. (Hons.) Oxon., Dip. Ed. (Oxon).
MRS. L. F. PLATT, B.A. (Hons.) Lond. Dip. Ed. (Cantab.)
(Nee Miss P. Ellis–Jones)

**OAKLEY HALL, OAKLEY, BASINGSTOKE,
HAMPSHIRE. Phone: Basingstoke 780222**

while exploring walks round Basingstoke. To prove that he was not altogether a paragon, he recalls the time he used to make bombs with gunpowder in old bottles and explode them in the old Canal, but one day one mis-fired and a friend got cut with flying glass, so the game was stopped. His Basingstoke was a place of long sunny afternoons, of roads still made of crushed flints very white and dusty in dry weather. He remembered seeing Queen Victoria just once, when the passengers were ushered off the platform at Basingstoke Station, and he saw, looking back, a grey haired old lady reading in one of the carriages. He was an interested observer of one of the first 'moving pictures' at the first cinema in the Corn Exchange, and of the X-rays demonstrated to a crowded audience in the Town Hall. In his day there were lamplighters with a long pole that somehow carried a little flame at the top, muffin men selling muffins from flat trays in the streets, milkmen selling milk from open buckets, dipped out with a measure on a long handle,

Members of the Basingstoke Cricket Club meeting at Mays Bounty.

the Town Crier with robe and cocked hat and a hoarse and husky voice. Mr Willis lived to be 92, and his collection of archaeological and historical objects became the foundation of the Willis Museum. Many, many people will remember Mr Willis with affection and respect for his kindness and his learning. His father was a watch and clock maker and jeweller in Wote Street, the shop is the small menswear shop now called Ashes. Mr Willis used to say it had been a public house, probably the Queens Head. He entered his father's business, later becoming a councillor, Alderman and, in 1923, the Mayor. In 1954 he was the first Freeman of the Borough. He was for many years Curator of the Willis Museum in New Street. This building was the first Mechanics Institute, begun to give working men a chance to get some further education. The institute was originally in Cross Street, and the new building was opened in 1869. Since the lectures given had titles like 'Mental Culture as a means of combating social backwardness and political despotism' it would seem that only the most determined thirster for education would have got much benefit from them.

Basingstoke passed through the nineteenth century getting

WE'VE GOT YOU SURROUNDED!

with FASTEX plastic fasteners, engineered assemblies and components for the Automotive, Home Appliance, Electronics, Caravanning, Sportsgoods, and Leisure Industries.

FASTEX

A DIVISION OF ITW LTD
VIABLES ESTATE, BASINGSTOKE, RG22 4BW
TEL: (0256) 461151 TELEX: 858801

Musselwhite employees, Hackwood House taken about 1906.

cleaner, lighter and was improved by public buildings and new schools. But there was a more primitive, violent Basingstoke, left over from the previous century. This is what happened in 1881.

The Salvation Army had set up a Headquarters in the old Silk Mill in Brook Street. They went on processions through the town, and preached against drunkenness, which was rather rash in a town like Basingstoke, which not only had May's Brewery, but two more, one at the end of Victoria Street owned by the Adams family, and another down Wote Street. Three Adams (Edward, Charles and Valentine) put out a bill asking men to meet in the Market Square to oppose the Salvation Army (which they called Dirty Dicks Army) on the following Sunday. As a result a large crowd met in the Square, and headed by the Adams, set off down Church Street, when the Army, intending to avoid them, turned into Church Square. The crowd was making a hideous noise and waving sticks, and it ran after the Salvationists, knocking them down and trampling and kicking them. After this horrifyingly violent attack, the Adams were summoned before a magistrate, but the case was dismissed. This was in May, 1881. In September there must have been more trouble, and since the gang could not get sureties they were sent to Winchester Gaol for two weeks. When they were released they returned in triumph, welcomed by hundreds with flags flying, and were given a dinner in the Corn Exchange and a silver watch apiece.

The Twentieth Century

During the Great War, soldiers were much in evidence in Basingstoke, for the first time since the Glorious Revolution of 1688. Both Fairfields and St John's schools were closed and taken over by the army, and soldiers were billeted on families in the town. Fairfields children went to Brook Street while St Johns boys went to the Queens School and the girls to classes in Church Cottage, but the 'sanitary arrangements' were not satisfactory and the school for the boys was very cold. Both schools were allowed back to their own premises in 1915.

Sometimes during these war years the children could not drill in their playground because the soldiers were marching by, creating

The Irish fusiliers at Basingstoke during the First World War, at the top of Sarum Hill opposite the Wheatsheaf.

clouds of dust, and the noise of their boots making it impossible for the children to hear the commands of their master. Roads were still roughly broken flints, and the dust in dry weather whitened the hedges.

There was no rationing in the 1914-18 war as there was in the Second World War, but there was voluntary rationing in 1918, causing long queues in shops. Thorneycrofts and Wallis and Steevens made 'munitions of War' according to the School Log, and their employees had high wages.

The inter-war years were generally a time of quiet prosperity for the people of the town. Aeroplanes were becoming a more common sight, but it must have been very exciting day when a famous pilot, Alan Cobham, who had made a name for his flights to India, South Africa and Australia, came to Basingstoke in 1929 and gave people trips in his 'plane.

Broadcasting started from London in 1922, but early sets were temperamental. Mr Willis remembered one of the first, that had to be controlled from a distance with long rods and there was a lot of interference. Later sets had valves instead of the 'crystal and cats whisker' that had been in the first sets, they had to be powered by large batteries that needed to be charged every week. When mains wireless came in St John's School had one, presented by the British Wire Broadcasting Service, Victoria Street Basingstoke.

For entertainment outside the home Basingstoke had four cinemas at one time, the Waldorf, now A.B.C., the Savoy which was on the opposite side of the Wote Street from A.B.C., by the precarious-looking house called Loddon Lodge, the Plaza which was originally the Drill Hall given by Col. John May, and the Grand, now the Haymarket Theatre. Pantomimes were also performed at the Grand.

Full time and Part Time Courses of Study available to cover all professions, skills and trades within the Departments of :-

Art and Design
Building
Business and Management Studies
Catering and Health Studies
General Studies
Technology

Basingstoke Technical College

Further details of course and enrolment always available from this College or telephone: Basingstoke 54141.

War work at Thorneycrofts in 1915.

During the 2nd World War Basingstoke was supposed to be a safe place. People who were bombed out of Portsmouth came here for shelter. The latest industry to come to the town, Eli Lilly, had to cover itself with camouflage because it was so conspicuous glaring white beside the railway. It had been floodlit at night and made much the same impact on Basingstoke as the A.A. building did in the 1960s. It was never hit but two sets of bombs did fall on Basingstoke, one in Church Square and Burgess Road, killing eleven people, in 1940. Later in the autumn another landed on a semi-detached house in Cliddesden Road, a private school.

Queen Mary's School moved away from Worting Road in 1940 to a much larger building at the top of Vyne Road. The old school was taken over by the Bank of England for a time, until the end of the war when it was rented by the County Council for £325 a year and finally sold to the County Council in 1947. It is now part of the Technial College.

In 1944 Sir Patrick Abercrombie put forward the Greater London Plan, which was to have far reaching consequences for Basingstoke. The Plan led to the New Towns Act of 1946 and the Town Development Act of 1952, which was to bring about the biggest change in the whole of the town's long history – its eventual choice as one of the New Towns.

The first choice of a New Town in Hampshire was Hook, one station nearer on the line to London. Hampshire County Council was violently opposed to the choice of Hook, for there would then have been continuous building from London right down to Basingstoke. Also there would have been drainage problems, but in fact Hampshire was against *any* new town in the county, for three large towns were already having to expand naturally (Bournemouth, Southampton and Portsmouth). They could not raise the objection that the land was excellent agricultural land, for it was mainly clay.

During the 1950s while the plans for a New Town were still at the discussion stage, land was available off Kingsclere Road and Winchester Road in Basingstoke, and many factories and industries were set up. Lansing Bagnall was one of the first.

In 1952 A.W.R.E Aldermaston had an estate built in the town for the employees of its new establishment in Aldermaston, most of them having come from London … these were the first of 'those people from London' so dreaded by Basingstoke, who turned out not to be so bad after all.

London and Hampshire County Councils next mooted Basingstoke and Andover as possible New Town sites, being ancient towns with excellent road and rail links to London and Southampton. The difficulties were that there was not quite enough land for the number of houses that would be needed, for Basingstoke alone had agreed to take 12,000 overspill already, and was to be required to take 30,000 in council houses and 8,000 in pri-

The Frame Gallery

(Proprietor: T. G. Toogood)

All work done on the premises

ARTWORK ORIGINALS AND LTD. EDITIONS

10 CHURCH STREET, BASINGSTOKE
HAMPSHIRE, TELEPHONE: (0256) 21088

G. Stevens newsagents and Lending Library at 25 Church Street, taken about 1923.

vate development (population of Basingstoke at the time was 17,000). The growth was planned to be from 26,000 to 76,000 over 15 years. There would need to be 16,000 new houses, 38 new schools, 15 churches and 500,000 sq feet of shopping space. Also new roads, drains, electricity and gas.

The houses had to be built at a 'high density' and some tall blocks were planned. Gardens were cut down in favour of community landscaping, but to the dismay of the planners, most people preferred a garden of their own. It must be said that the trees, open spaces and flower-planting are splendid, and the high banks cut off a good deal of the noise from the roads that tore through the old fields that had been around the town. The amazing plan of a platform from just outside the railway station right across the valley to the top of the town, to carry shops, car parks and pedestrian walks, produced 272 objections when it was shown in 1962.

Possibly the main feelings were emotional rather than rational, for it was an immense step to take, but there had been changes that would have had to be made even if no new town was to be built.

The roads through the town were too narrow and the shops too small for the traffic and the trade that was bound to come (the recession was not foreseen, apparently, in the 1960s). The *Gazette* printed many letters for and against the plan, protest meetings boiled up around the town, the arguments being (1) the cost to the ratepayers, (2) the probable trouble that 'people from London' would cause, (3) the destruction of the whole centre of the town and (4) the compensation for the removal of shops and homes by the development. For the plan, there were voices claiming that the shops of Basingstoke were scanty in stocks, slow in service and closed at lunch-times, that the roads were terrible, the rates would be supported by grants and loans from London, and that new blood was wanted.

But the new town was built, and for ten years there was mud on the roads and the continual thud of the pile-driving machines as

Church Street about 1955. To the left were shops, St John's School, a pub named The Self Defence, the Methodist Church, Queen Anne House, Bedford House and the Conservative Club.

they made the land at the bottom of the town where the Loddon ran, called 'putty chalk', safe to carry the platform. When it was done a rather impressive wall ran along the east side of Church Street, over which it would not have been surprising to see the noses of cannon, and the new shops opened on top. Around the town new estates spread out, new bus routes extended, and the new Basingstoke emerged, with a current population of 90,000.

The estates around the town house most of the inhabitants. They are, going north from the Station, South View, Oakridge and Popley. Popley is a good half hour's walk and not much less by bus from the Town Centre. To the west, Winklebury north of the railway, south of it Buckskin and South Ham. Just to the north of the M3 is Brighton Hill. Along to the east of Brighton Hill are Ruckstalls and Black Dam and across the old London Road is Riverdene. Each estate is a little village in itself with a shopping centre, infant, junior

Church Street following development.

and secondary schools of its own, a community centre that can sometimes be a church on Sundays, and a public house. There are playing fields and one piece of land (Crabtree Plantation) has been kept for youth organisations to use for camping or field study, with a Nature Reserve close by. Eastrop Park has a paddling pool and two other larger ponds, for rowing and model boats. The Memorial Park has avenues of large old trees and two grass arenas which come into their own in Fair Week, when a Fun Fair is set up in one and displays and shows are in the other. A procession goes through the town on the Thursday of Fair Week and ends in the Park Arena. For the rest of the year it is a pleasant place to walk round under the trees, and there are tennis courts as well.

In the Town Centre is the Sports Centre where there are two swimming pools and four squash courts, a large sports hall and other smaller places to play almost any game you can mention. There are very varied opportunities for employment. The official guide from the Council Offices has eleven pages listing the names and addresses of firms and their businesses. It would be unfair to pick out only a few from all these. They are in districts set apart for factories; one between Kingsclere Road and the Railway, (Hound-mills) Daneshill, between Reading Road and the railway on the east, Viables, to the south-west of the town, Thorneycroft Industrial estate off Worting Road and Percy Bilton off Winchester Road.

The ABC Cinema near the New Market Place has two screens, and there is a theatre in Wote Street, the Haymarket, the old Corn Exchange, now re-built and enlarged. Out at West Ham is a Lido and a small golf course. Horses are no longer raced on the Down. There are two Market Places, one where the market has always

WYATT'S BLINDS

We supply:

Blinds, Curtain Tracks/Poles and Curtains
Measuring and Fitting Service.
Manufacturers of all types of blinds and awnings

21, LONDON ST. BASINGSTOKE. Tel: (0256) 50051

Pedestrianised London Street in 1980. By courtesy of the Basingstoke and Deane Borough Council.

been, and the other next to the Bus Station. Market days are Wednesday and Saturday, and fruit and vegetables are the things sold in the main, but a great variety of other items are sold too.

In the Library, which is large and light and spacious, there are notice-boards with information about the many clubs and organisations that exist, and a Citizens Advice Bureau. Help can be found in the Consumers Advice Bureau and if you are really in despair there is a branch of Samaritans. All the doctors have surgeries in the Health Centre in Bramblys Grange, which is rather out of the way in a small road off Winchester Road. An immense Hospital has been built to replace the tiny Hackwood Road Hospital. The new hospital is right away from the town, almost in Sherborne St John, sharing grounds with Park Prewett Hospital which deals with mental illness.

Buses run all round the town, but the town centre is for pedestrians only. There is also a taxi rank just off the New Market Square, which is helpful to the housewife going home laden from the super-

Basingstoke Town Centre. Shoppers are watching the arrival of the new Beaujolais by Shire horse and cart. By courtesy of the Basingstoke and Deane Borough Council.

market.

Because of the plan to keep the centre of the town free of traffic, there is a big car park partly beside and partly above the shopping centre. Deliveries are made below the platform or from newly made back roads in the streets that are not on the shopping platform. To avoid having to cross roads, pedestrians have to use subways (or bridges) which means that it is not always possible to get straight to the place one hopes to reach and it is all rather like 'Alice through the Looking Glass', one may have to go almost in the opposite direction to get where one aims to be.

Basingstoke has come a very long way from the lonely hunters, the fierce tribes of invaders, serfs, burgesses and loyal men of Basingstoke. There are still some 'sturdy rogues' about and some 'fighting, chiding and heads breaking' but in the main the men and women of Basingstoke today have what the Englishman always wanted, a house and garden of his own and peace in which to enjoy them.

Further Reading

Those who wish to extend their reading may find the following books listed below of interest:

Around Basingstoke	A. Attwood
Look into the Past	A. Attwood
History of Basingstoke	Baigent & Millard
Love Loyalty	Wilf Emberton
Queen Mary's School	
1556-1972	E.G. Stokes & R.C. Crossman
Wallis & Steevens, a History	R.A. Whitehead
The Dream Fulfilled	ed. Brendan Butler
Voices of Basingstoke	A. Hawker

The following may be consulted at the Hampshire Record Office, Winchester:
Court Rolls 1386-1491
Court Book 1503-1522
Rentals 1400-1841
Charity Accounts 1754-1820
Examinations before Justices 1653-1718
Payments at Courts 1423-1841
Vestry Records 1698-1833
Wills 1500-1650

Probably the Best Costumes in the South.
Make–up and Accessories also available.
Send S.A.E. **Free** Brochures.

FANCY DRESS

UNIT 3, UPPER WOTE ST. Tel: BASINGSTOKE (0256) 29624

Index